MW01165714

Experience God

In Nature and The Bible

Original Poems in

Contemporary Rhyming Verse

Written by

Dr. Rick L. Williams

Includes Color Photographs and

Bible Verses from the King James Version

i

Rick L. Williams, Ph.D.

Scripture references quoted are taken from The King James Version (KJV) of The Bible and are intended to provide increased devotion for each original inspirational poem written.

ISBN-13: 978-1500810870
ISBN-10: 1500810878
Library of Congress Control Number 2013914825
Createspace, Amazon Books Publishing Co.
North Charleston, South Carolina

DEDICATION

This book is dedicated to God,
my family, church, and friends who all inspire me.

Throughout my life I've enjoyed many walks with God to talk about the plans that we have made. God has always been right there to encourage me and to give me love. He's always been right there to show the way. Discover God with me as I walk with Him in the mountains, on the farm, and along the sea.

FORWARD POEM

As I Walked Along with God

In the mountains, on the farm,
And along the shining sea,
I heard God's voice, he called, and then
He walked along with me.

I heard it just as plain as day
And in the dark of night,
He spoke to me through all I heard,
And never left my sight.

(Poem Continues)

Job 39:8 King James Version (KJV)
8 The range of the mountains is his pasture,
And he searcheth after every green thing.

The mountains filled with all the sounds
Of mammals, birds, and bees,
As we walked, they chirped and swooped on by
And flew throughout the trees.

I heard and saw an eagle fly,
A magnificent sight to see.
Their voices sang a nice refrain,
To God's own chat with me.

(Poem Continues)

Rick L. Williams, Ph.D.

Psalm 65:12 King James Version (KJV)
12 They drop upon the pastures of the wilderness,
And the little hills rejoice on every side.

In farms we walked along the fields
To eye the bounty there,
And I heard farm horses, cows, and sheep,
Their voices in the air.

The rooster crowed, a dog barked loud,
And crows, they filled the sky.
The rainbow trout were silent; but
They splashed and swam on by.

(Poem Continues)

Along the sea, the waves crashed by,
And seagulls beckoned me.
We walked the beach, the clouds blew in,
And crabs ran busily.

The ocean's deep, the water's blue,
The horizon's far away,
God's voice called me to chat with Him
On this and every day.

Ecclesiastes 3:11 King James Version (KJV)
11 He hath made every thing beautiful in his time: also
he hath set the world in their heart, so that no man can
find out the work that God maketh from the beginning to
the end.

http://www.facebook.com/drlovepoems

ACKNOWLEDGMENTS

I would like to acknowledge my loving wife Lynda, who has shared my adventures in life, including helping me to copy edit this new inspirational book of poems, based on my own real-life experiences and my personal walk with God.

Lynda has also faithfully supported my work with the first book that I have written in this four-book series on Greek Love: <u>Romantic Poems, Right From The Heart</u>.

She has been a constant source of love and support in my many author-reading and book-signing events.

I would like to thank North Brunswick, NJ Public Library, where I organized these manuscripts, as well as the Bristol, RI and North Brunswick libraries that have ordered and cataloged my books. Thanks also go to Amazon.com for their support in publishing my books in paperback as well as in Kindle editions.

I would like to thank Barnes & Noble, in Middletown, RI and North Brunswick, NJ--and many other florists, restaurants, and store venues for the opportunities to hold author book presentations in real brick-and-mortar stores, as well as stock and sell my books. Thank you to many other bookstores in 12 countries around the world who stock and sell my publications.

Rick L. Williams, Ph.D.

Psalm 36:6 King James Version (KJV)
6 Thy righteousness is like the great mountains; thy judgments are a great deep: O Lord, thou preservest man and beast.

TABLE OF CONTENTS

CHAPTER 1 of 3

I WALKED WITH GOD
IN THE MOUNTAINTOPS

Psalm 65:13 King James Version(KJV)
13 The pastures are clothed with flocks; the valleys also
are covered over with corn; they shout for joy, they also
sing.

TABLE OF CONTENTS

CHAPTER 2 of 3

I WALKED WITH GOD
DOWN ON THE FARM

Rick L. Williams, Ph.D.

1 Kings 4:29 (King James Version)
29 And God gave Solomon wisdom and understanding exceeding much; and largeness of heart, even as the sand that is on the sea shore.

TABLE OF CONTENTS

CHAPTER 3 of 3

I WALKED WITH GOD
ALONG THE SEA

Rick L. Williams, Ph.D.

Isaiah 52:7 King James Version (KJV)
7 How beautiful upon the mountains are the feet of him
that bringeth good tidings, that publisheth peace; that
bringeth good tidings of good, that publisheth salvation;
that saith unto Zion, Thy God reigneth!

CHAPTER 1

I WALKED WITH GOD

IN THE MOUNTAINTOPS

God's Mountaintops

Majestic mountains pierce the air,
Like God's own grandeur standing there,
They rise above, immensely grand,
Agape sentinels of the land.

The woodland forest with field and stream,
Gives rise to rock-faced precipices.
In sharp contrast to woodland ferns,
The mountain cliffs are rough and stern.

For many living down below,
The mountains hold great truths untold.
The peaks inspire us all to climb,
And forge through life in God's due time.

(Poem Continues)

Amidst the strife of life embraced,
Big streams we ford and rainbows chase.
Till in the quiet mountaintops,
We find God's peace and anguish stops.

Big dreams appear in moments then,
When we can rest and clear our heads.
The vision's clear, we know our place,
Above the clouds in God's own face.

Psalm 72:3 King James Version (KJV)
3 The mountains shall bring peace to the people, and the
little hills, by righteousness.

Rick L. Williams, Ph.D.

God's Voice

The mountains brought God's voice to me,
In quiet moments of serenity.
No human noise befuddled now
The voice of God that spoke right out.

God's voice called out to me I swear
From every rock and stream right there.
Reminding me, He called my name
To listen now without disdain.

He spoke through all the birds and bees
That sang and buzzed all through the trees.
From every rock and fallen log
His voice spoke out, and sang a song:

(Poem Continues)

Deuteronomy 28:2 King James Version (KJV)
2 And all these blessings shall come on thee, and overtake thee, if thou shalt hearken unto the voice of the Lord thy God.

Isaiah 44:23 King James Version (KJV)

23 Sing, O ye heavens; for the Lord hath done it: shout, ye lower parts of the earth: break forth into singing, ye mountains, O forest, and every tree therein: for the Lord hath redeemed Jacob, and glorified himself in Israel.

Experience God

"Come closer now and be my friend,
My endless love will know no end.
For I have made all this and you,
Created life and all is good.

"Your place is here I hope you see.
So come right near and speak to me.
I'll listen always, what's your intent?
I am your guide, that's Heaven sent.

"Tell me now just what you feel,
And know for sure my love is real.
Walk through the pines, my forest church.
It's filled with needles, cones, and birch."

(Poem Continues)

"Explain to me your thoughts and dreams,
The challenges you face and all your schemes.
And if you are quite quiet too,
I'll even gently speak to you.

"With reassuring love I'm found
In every passing bird and cloud.
Please learn to place your trust in me.
I will provide just what you need.

"And as you go along your way,
I'll be right near, so always stay
Quite close and simply talk to me,
Your friend, your God--eternally."

Psalm 76:4 King James Version (KJV)
4 Thou art more glorious and excellent than the
mountains of prey.

My Secret Summer Waterfalls

I hiked alone in the woods with God,
As a boy of twelve, it seems,
And on this hike--a short journey,
Was God, the woods, and me.

And as I traveled far that day
Past deer and birds that sing,
I spied a summer waterfalls
That came out from a spring.

I ran right up to the waterfalls
That rushed over hills on the ground,
I peered over rocks and logs, and yelled,.
"Look God what I've found!"

(Poem Continues)

A hidden secret waterfalls
Had somehow come my way.
God laughed and then was smiling.
For He knew it was there all day.

It sure was very hot outside,
So I decided to jump right in.
The waterfalls rushed over me,
And uplifted my soul within.

Psalm 42:7 King James Version (KJV)
7 Deep caller unto deep at the noise of thy waterspouts:
all thy waves and thy billows are gone over me.

Skyline Drive

I journeyed up the mountainside,
To God's highway--called Skyline Drive.
The beauty that surrounded me
Surpassed my dreams--exceedingly.

At first the climb was slow in pace,
Past Shenandoah's entrance gate.
Winding turns they took me through,
As wondrous sights came into view.

God's birds now came alive with song.
The butterflies just came along.
A rabbit hopped, a deer pranced by,
A bear just stared and wondered why.

(Poem Continues)

The road grew steep as I drove on.
Some rocks had fallen by a log.
Then much to my surprise the bend
Went down and then back up again.

A roller-coaster ride it seemed,
With twists and turns as sunlight gleamed
Among the trees, it dimmed quite low,
But broke right out on edges though.

(Poem Continues)

Mark 3:13 King James Version (KJV)

13 And he goeth up into a mountain, and calleth unto him whom he would: and they came unto him.

Rick L. Williams, Ph.D.

Psalm 11:1 King James Version (KJV)
11 In the Lord put I my trust: how say ye to my soul, Flee
as a bird to your mountain?

Experience God

The overlooks on every turn,
Had views so grand for eyes to learn
What lies below the far beyond:
Each village, stream, each lake and pond.

As each new turn came into view,
I looked about to see what's new.
The distant dots that once were huge
Seemed tiny now amidst the blue.

(Poem Continues)

Till nothing from before at all
Was seen; no buildings, lakes, or falls.
Just clouds as they came sweeping by
And filled the distant mountain skies.

Another world as seldom seen
By those who live below the trees.
To Heaven's heights where Angels fly
God's mountain highway--called Skyline Drive.

Psalm 48:1 King James Version (KJV)
48 Great is the Lord, and greatly to be praised in the city of our God, in the mountain of his holiness.

Rick L. Williams, Ph.D.

Psalm 55:8 King James Version (KJV)
8 I would hasten my escape from the windy storm and tempest.

Mighty Wicked Mountain Storm

A mighty wicked mountain storm
Blew in last night and surprised us all.
Great streaks of lightning filled the sky,
As thunderous downpours left nothing dry.

Then thunder claps, they shook the ground
For a hundred miles all around!
So loud, our screams seemed all in vain,
Above the noise of torrential rain.

A mighty wicked mountain storm
Made rivers of the forest floor.
And helpless on the mountaintop,
We prayed to God for it to stop!

(Poem Continues)

But it showed no sign of slowing down.
Instead more lightning struck the ground!
And giant lightning cracks were sent
It seemed like daggers to kill us dead!

At last the storm had set us free.
And moved away past landslide trees.
We raised our voices to God in praise!
For morning dawned with sunlit rays.

Isaiah 29:6 King James Version (KJV)
6 Thou shalt be visited of the Lord of hosts with thunder, and with earthquake, and great noise, with storm and tempest.

Luke 21:36 King James Version (KJV)
36 Watch ye therefore, and pray always, that ye may be accounted worthy to escape all these things that shall come to pass, and to stand before the Son of man.

Tunnel Through the Mountainside

A tunnel through the mountainside
Appeared in front of me.
And it looked dark and dangerous
As far as I could see.

But I was on a mountain cliff
With no other way around.
If I turned to the right or left
I'd plummet to the ground.

The ground below this mountainside
Was thousands of feet below.
And I could see a storm behind,
The winds began to blow.

The lightning struck and rain it fell
In torrents on the road.
So I moved forward cautiously
Into the great unknown.

Then half way through I saw a light
Appear in front of me.
The end of the tunnel was now in view
With sunshine for all to see.

The Great Smoky Mountains

The sunrise breaks through clouds of white.
A new day dawns from storms last night.
The Great Smoky Mountains now earn their name,
As white smoke billows across the chain.

Like chimney stacks, the smoke pours out
From mountain streams, past rainbow trout.
To greet the sky as morning dew
Gives way to mountain scenic views.

Endless chains of mountaintops,
Far as the eye can see--it pops.
The woods filled full of teeming life,
The pheasants, deer, rabbits, and mice.

And kinfolk who live in the holler
Grandma, Grandpa, Ma, and Father.
They keep a watch on all the kids,
Their chores with water, wood, and pigs.

They keep the faith where God is strong,
And praise His glory with bluegrass songs.
The banjo, guitar, mouth harp, and spoons,
Keep rhythm with their gospel tunes.

John 6:3 King James Version (KJV)
3 And Jesus went up into a mountain, and there he sat with his disciples.

Cavern Waterfalls

I walked one day through woodland trees,
Past rocks and streams and flowers with bees.
In a cool damp breeze, I heard God's call
From a small entrance in a mountain wall.

I heard a rushing sound within,
And despite the dark, I crawled right in.
Then shining a light in front of me
I spied stalactites hanging precariously.

Colorful formations now grew so tall.
And stone curtains hung from every wall.
Giant columns stood by guardedly,
Incredible beauty God made for me.

(Poem Continues)

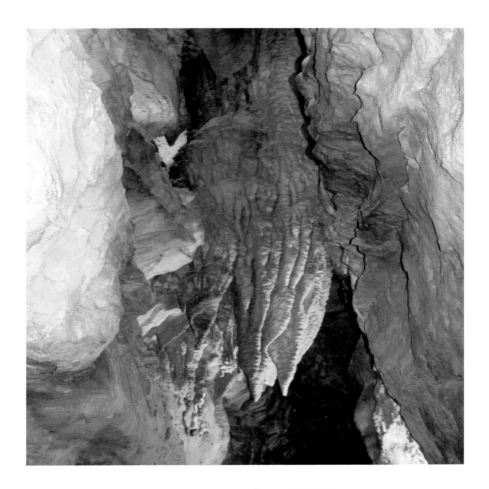

Mark 6:29 King James Version (KJV)
29 And when his disciples heard of it, they came and took up his corpse, and laid it in a tomb.

John 4:14 King James Version (KJV)
14 But whosoever drinketh of the water that I shall give him shall never thirst; but the water that I shall give him shall be in him a well of water springing up into everlasting life.

Experience God

A swift cool breeze went sweeping by,
As rushing torrents fell from high.
A magnificent wonderful hidden surprise
And I could hardly believe my eyes.

I walked right up to that underground delight.
The room was huge, the ceiling: out of sight!
And bending my head to God, after all,
He surprised me with a cavern waterfalls.

Rick L. Williams, Ph.D.

A Hike with God

I took a hike with God today,
Along a trail that came my way.
The mountain trail had many rocks,
With time to walk and think a lot.

We forded streams and fallen logs,
And crossed large fields laid thick with fog.
Into the forest hills we climbed,
But God's a steady mountain guide.

My hikes with God taught lifelong lessons.
To respect all things and count my blessings.
I learned to have a heart that's strong,
And admit when I've done something wrong.

This hike along the mountain trail
Brought us to rocks so steep and bare.
But views below where we have run
Showed all the distance we have come.

Life's lessons are often hard at times.
Just like the hikes that we have climbed.
But God on hikes; He reminded me
He blesses us and sets us free!

Deuteronomy 33:15 King James Version (KJV)
15 And for the chief things of the ancient mountains, and
for the precious things of the lasting hills,

Rick L. Williams, Ph.D.

A Bear That Startled Me

As I enjoyed a midday snack
Along a mountain view,
A bear came up and startled me,
So what was I to do?

The bear seemed big and huge to me,
Seven or eight feet long.
I snapped his picture without a flash
On my android phone.

But as the bear walked closer now
And headed straight for me,
To my car I walked, still facing him
A little more speedily.

(Poem Continues)

The bear, he didn't growl or run.
He'd really done nothing wrong.
I think he was just curious
To see if I belonged.

But into my car, I went real quick!
A convertible with the top still down!
And fumbling with my keys and brakes,
I pressed the pedal down!

Genesis 1:25 King James Version (KJV)
25 And God made the beast of the earth after his kind, and cattle after their kind, and every thing that creepeth upon the earth after his kind: and God saw that it was good.

Psalm 27:14 King James Version (KJV)
14 Wait on the Lord: be of good courage, and he shall strengthen thine heart: wait, I say, on the Lord.

Dangerous Zip-Line Ride

I went on a dangerous zip-line ride
Above the Smokies: 7,000 feet high!
My harness suspended from a dangling chain
On a wheel of steel, which was totally insane!

For when the guide had let me go,
I picked up speed out of control.
First 20, then 40, and 60 MPH,
To slow down, my hand's the brake!

In a leather glove; with a hard-curved center
Across a steel cable: 100 yards or better.
I had to pull down on the cable or I'd crash
Into the platform, where my brains would be smashed!

(Poem Continues)

Rick L. Williams, Ph.D.

I tried to look around and spy
The mountains below, before I soon died!
But the wheel on my harness to my horror I found
Kept turning me around, and around, and around.

I let go the brake hand, to steady the thing,
Then firmly grasped and turned the D-ring.
To gain control of the direction I'm in
I used all my might to turn the small thing!

And to regain control of my forward descent
I still had to reach up and hand brake again.
Remember, no fingers in front of the wheel!
Or they soon will be chopped off and spit out: for real!

(Poem Continues)

Isaiah 3:18 King James Version (KJV)
18 In that day the Lord will take away the bravery of
their tinkling ornaments about their feet, and their cauls,
and their round tires like the moon,

I looked up and placed my hand on that line,
Across the bottom cable; just barely in time
To slow my descent to the platform below,
Where people were yelling and shouting to go!

Finally, I made it intact and okay!
And I asked the dear Lord, "Why I came, anyway?"
I had survived zip-lining death this one last time.
Then I remembered, there were six more zip lines!

Habakkuk 3:19 King James Version (KJV)
19 The Lord God is my strength, and he will make my feet like hinds' feet, and he will make me to walk upon mine high places. To the chief singer on my stringed instruments.

Rick L. Williams, Ph.D.

Sunsets and Stargazing

I went stargazing past streams and rocks,
Up winding roads to mountaintops.
Man's businesses faded from view,
From cities, towns, and farmlands too.

A quietness, it filled the place.
No mention from the human race.
But then I heard a symphony
Of wind and birds sweep through the trees.

God's orchestrated nightly scene
Began as mountain sunsets gleamed.
First clouds of white were blowing by,
Now red and pink lit up the sky.

(Poem Continues)

Deuteronomy 4:19 King James Version (KJV)
19 And lest thou lift up thine eyes unto heaven, and
when thou seest the sun, and the moon, and the stars,
even all the host of heaven, shouldest be driven to
worship them, and serve them, which the Lord thy God
hath divided unto all nations under the whole heaven.

At first, all mixed in skies of blue,
The colors, bright, faded from view,
Then twinkling lights appeared on high
Over darkened ground and blackened sky.

Silent stars appeared, a few,
Then many more came into view,
Until the Heavens were lit up bright
With dazzling dots of God's starlight.

I was amazed to see and know
God's sky displayed a nighttime show.
For as I lay there looking now,
The stars, they danced and fell somehow.

Across the sky I tried to count
The stars and planets all about.
But billions now, for so it seemed
Brightly filled this evening scene.

(Poem Continues)

Genesis 1:16 King James Version (KJV)
16 And God made two great lights; the greater light to rule the day, and the lesser light to rule the night: he made the stars also.

A dazzling, sparkling spectacle,
A universe so bright and full.
God's Alpha and Omega--without end,
Past Earth, the Moon, and Sun extend.

A wondrous glimpse afforded me
On this mountaintop, above the trees.
Those comets, moons, and planets far,
God shows to us from where we are.

And now man travels among the stars,
With rockets, cameras, and robot arms,
But I still enjoy Earth's mountain place
Where I can go and see God's face.

Job 22:12 King James Version (KJV)
12 Is not God in the height of heaven? And behold the height of the stars, how high they are!

Job 39:8 King James Version (KJV)
8 The range of the mountains is his pasture, and he searcheth after every green thing.

CHAPTER 2

I WALKED WITH GOD

DOWN ON THE FARM

Psalm 23:2 King James Version (KJV)
2 He maketh me to lie down in green pastures: he leadeth
me beside the still waters.

Patchwork Quilts

The farmland's covered like a patchwork quilt.
With big red barns and cornfield silk.
Horse-drawn buggies travel along,
Where crops grow tall and birds sing songs.

There's an endless sea of hay and corn,
Intertwining roads all worn.
Women bake and quilt bedspreads.
Men plow fields and fences mend.

(Poem Continues)

Cows feed on grass and find cool shade.
The land's now rich with smells they've made.
The aroma's strong all through the air,
With fertilized soil and crops grown there.

The shepherds, busy tending flocks,
Farmers raise their kids and crops.
The patchwork farms, they so endear,
Make life complete on farmlands here.

Farmlands provide a wholesome life
Without the hassles of city strife.
Sustaining families, faith, and kin,
Are patchwork lands these farms are in.

Isaiah 64:8 King James Version (KJV)
8 But now, O Lord, thou art our father; we are the clay,
and thou our potter; and we all are the work of thy hand.

Rick L. Williams, Ph.D.

God Grew up on a Farm with Me

God grew up on a farm with me.
A simple life where I was free.
And I knew he was always there,
I talked with him most everywhere.

He walked with me right down the lane
To our old farmhouse, past tall tree shade.
God's creatures were there living too.
They swam in streams, crawled by, or flew.

I'm told God's present everywhere,
But I found God in that country air.
He helped me plant the summer corn,
And pick the produce all day long.

(Poem Continues)

Psalm 79:13 King James Version (KJV)
13 So we thy people and sheep of thy pasture will give thee thanks for ever: we will shew forth thy praise to all generations.

We had tomatoes, carrots, and peas,
Pumpkins, squash, and strawberries.
He made it grow from tiny seeds.
I only helped to pull the weeds.

God rode bareback on a horse with me,
As mooing cows chomped hungrily.
One time we made a chicken run,
And God fell down! He laughed from fun.

(Poem Continues)

Psalm 95:7 King James Version (KJV)
7 For he is our God; and we are the people of his pasture, and the sheep of his hand. Today if ye will hear his voice,

He was there in discoveries made.
Even that skunk that sprayed and sprayed!
God ran along with my dog and I,
And helped me up when I fell and cried.

A child's delight to have such a friend
Like God--my pal--my confidant.
We laughed and played all day on the farm,
And He made sure I met no harm.

For my God--my pal, knows all you see,
My hurts, and pains, and what's tickling me.
It's great to have a friend like God,
When you're lucky enough to grow up on a farm.

Psalm 65:12 King James Version (KJV)
12 They drop upon the pastures of the wilderness: and
the little hills rejoice on every side.

Rick L. Williams, Ph.D.

Cornfields

The cornfields, they go on and on
Past every road and farmer's barn.
A sea of stalks all standing tall,
Row after row, through summer and fall.

There is no end to what you see,
These fields of corn run endlessly.
They fill your view of farmlands rich
On every valley, and hill, and ditch.

A ride throughout this countryside
With fields of corn that fill your eyes.
In farmland quilts, across the land
Of farmer's dirt and fields, expand.

(Poem Continues)

The giant ears of golden corn
Grow on the stalks, the silk adorns.
The tiny kernels inside the husks,
A hidden treat for all of us.

A symbol of God's bounty grown,
The stalks in bundles by our homes
Are used to decorate the halls
Of farmland harvest festivals.

Genesis 27:28 King James Version (KJV)
28 Therefore God give thee of the dew of heaven, and the fatness of the earth, and plenty of corn and wine:

Rick L. Williams, Ph.D.

Genesis 26:30 King James Version (KJV)
30 And he made them a feast, and they did eat and drink.

Smorgasbord

I went to a farmer's Smorgasbord
Among the farms and fields of corn,
Which I could very plainly see,
Outside the window in front of me.

All freshly picked, sliced, steamed, and baked,
The farmers' produce, meat, and cakes,
These foods to fill our hunger pains
Were now laid out in big buffets.

Some apple butter and fresh coleslaw,
Carrots, lettuce, peas for all,
Cottage cheese, and tomatoes red,
All healthy things to keep us fed.

Sliced roasted pork, potatoes, ham,
Corned beef and cabbage, steak, and lamb.
Endless foods that delight your eyes,
Desserts galore and shoofly pie.

There's just no end and plenty more
For starving people run in their doors,
But they're slow in leaving: no room for more
At *all-you-can-eat* smorgasbords.

Rick L. Williams, Ph.D.

Farmer's Market

The farmer's market is like Heaven to me
It's filled with some fruit, corn, and many a treat,
There are celery, tomatoes, and pies made of peach,
Potatoes, green beans, and strawberries to eat.

The rhubarb is tart, but with sugar tastes fine.
There are apples, cider, and an assortment of wines.
Brown sugar and molasses are in shoofly pies,
Homemade cinnamon buns and lemon meringue pies.

The hard candy is sweet, there are jellies in jars,
And tables covered with chocolate Hershey bars.
Licorice sticks and cough drops are sold,
To sooth your sore throat if you have a cold.

(Poem Continues)

There is cookware complete with ironclad feel,
Utensils and knives, all forged in bright steel.
The pottery cups and the stoneware are good
For enjoying God's meals made of all this great food.

Handmade quilts and baskets abound,
To show all the crafting and skills that are found.
I love farmer's markets and the fruits of the land.
The farmers are friendly and everything's grand.

Genesis 6:21 King James Version (KJV)
21 And take thou unto thee of all food that is eaten, and
thou shalt gather it to thee; and it shall be for food for
thee, and for them.

Isaiah 30:23 King James Version (KJV)
23 Then shall he give the rain of thy seed, that thou shalt sow the ground withal; and bread of the increase of the earth, and it shall be fat and plenteous: in that day shall thy cattle feed in large pastures.

Planting Seeds

The fields God's farmers harrow--as we turn up the land,
Are planted with His seeds, all that we can.
We uncover the blessed truth of God's Holy Light,
And lean on His Son, each day and every night.

We water the fields of crops that for miles expand,
In God's fertile soil, the rows He commands.
We strengthen our human spirit with God's great discern,
And share His great love with those who would learn.

Our crops stand tall when they grow so you can see,
Our hard work is rewarded with God's great bounty.
We're proud true believers; we follow His truth
He's asked us to share with others like you.

Now it's the great harvest at last come for us,
We reap the ripe corn and peel back the husks.
We'll share the great news of God from above,
So others can accept the truth of His love.

The food that's harvested is shared by one and all,
However it's big or however it's small,
God's greatest gift is that of Jesus, His Son.
Redemption and love are meant for everyone.

Psalm 32:9 King James Version (KJV)
9 Be ye not as the horse, or as the mule, which have no understanding: whose mouth must be held in with bit and bridle, lest they come near unto thee.

Country Wagon Ride

A wagon ride into the countryside,
An Amish horse-drawn buggy ride.
Straw hats for shade, handmade girls' bonnets,
Reciting prayers and lovely verse sonnets.

Now snap the reins hard, the horses move fast.
25 miles per hour, the trees rush past.
Leather straps, they carry the heavy load,
They sway and bounce as we travel along the road.

Sweet smells of fragrant meadows I suppose,
Fill my head through the nostrils of my nose.
The odor coming from horse and cow manure,
We've learned to love or simply just ignore.

(Poem Continues)

Rick L. Williams, Ph.D.

Reminds us of the richness of kin,
Of hard work done and many blessings.
Enjoying the richest land on Earth,
We praise our God for all He's worth.

The landscaped farms and silos seen,
A farmer's delight--a lifelong dream.
To till the land and grow up our crops,
An endless endeavor--the work never stops.

John 6:35 King James Version (KJV)
35 And Jesus said unto them, I am the bread of life: he
that cometh to me shall never hunger; and he that
believeth on me shall never thirst.

Paradise

A farm is a country paradise, loved by God I'm told.
Feeding many people when their crops are *bought-n-sold*.
I know God loves the farmer and the farmer's family too.
They toil in the fields all day to bring His food to you.

Farm life is quite simple, yet it's also very grand.
Farmers find its beauty in the lay of the land.
The work is very hard, yet they still have time for fun
When chores are all finished and the workday is done.

In simple things farmers find their God's endless love,
Among friends and family they are snug as a bug.
Taking simple pleasure in growing things for you,
Giving praise for sunshine and the rain that comes by too.
(Poem Continues)

Luke 23:43 King James Version (KJV)
43 And Jesus said unto him, Verily I say unto thee, today shalt thou be with me in paradise.

Rick L. Williams, Ph.D.

Farmers spend a lot of time in God's Holy Word,
They tend the crops well and shepherd all the herds.
They all know how to dance and to sing a gospel tune,
They're also great at romance; under God's full moon.

The harvest is God's plenty, it's a celebration of life,
A farmer's paradise--a harvester's delight.
Their towns named Blue Ball, Bird-In-Hand, and Lititz,
Intercourse and Paradise; well their names really fit.

Revelation 2:7 King James Version (KJV)
7 He that hath an ear, let him hear what the Spirit saith unto the churches; To him that overcometh will I give to eat of the tree of life, which is in the midst of the paradise of God.

Rick L. Williams, Ph.D.

Swimming Hole--Down by the Creek

Down on the farm, when it gets really hot,
We cool off our heels at our favorite swimming spot,
Down to our swimming hole we very often streak
To laugh and swim endlessly, and frolic in the creek.

First we call our cousins, "Please come right now!
Come quickly to the creek, and don't forget a towel.
Bring your swimming trunks and some tire inner tubes.
Down to the creek where the water's really cool.

Go on down that old farm road and travel for a while,
Past the barn and silo, a trip about two miles.
It winds all around, so at the fork: stay left
Past cows, the pigs, and horses: then head due west.

You'll see us swimming playfully at water creek.
Please come quickly now--be fast upon your feet,
We have a rope tied on a tree, right there upon the hill.
Tightly grasp the rope and swing, it's really quite a thrill.

When you swing out far let go and jump into the creek.
Then give us all a Tarzan yell and we'll join in to shriek.
We'll picnic there as well, with lots of food piled high:
Cornbread and chicken; and for dessert Mom's apple pie.

Proverbs 18:24 King James Version (KJV)
24 A man that hath friends must shew himself friendly:
and there is a friend that sticketh closer than a brother.

God's Kicking Boots Down on the Farm

I danced with God down on the farm,
And He sang along with me.
But did you know God plays in a bluegrass band?
His fiddle can't be beat.

God dances up quite a storm,
When it comes to square dance tunes.
He's great at hoedown do-si-dos.
God knows all the steps of the Cotton-Eyed Joe.

God and I called a square dance song.
We've been practicing for three months long,
We stood right up and called commands,
To squares of dancers hand in hand.

(Poem Continues)

God told me now, "You call with country soul.
'You've Got to Have an Ace in the Hole'."
While we both taught those line-dance dudes,
God ws slapping leather and kicking country boots!

The night I did hoedowns in the barn with God,
My country square dance singing, it made Him proud.
I learned it's okay, when you're down on the farm
To dance with God, in the hay, in the barn.

Psalm 149:3 King James Version (KJV)
3 Let them praise his name in the dance: let them sing
praises unto him with the timbrel and harp.

1 Samuel 14:25 King James Version (KJV)
25 And all they of the land came to a wood; and there
was honey upon the ground.

Lightning Bugs and Bumblebees

Lightning bugs and bumblebees,
A kid's idea to capture these,
In big glass jars, I swooped them up,
These fireflies and buzzing bugs.

I'd run across the fields at dusk
And scoop those bugs that lit right up
Into a jar with twigs and leaves,
And tiny holes on top to breathe.

Until the jar became quite full
Of fireflies to light my room.
So I could stay up late at night
To read comics by their nightlights.

And then one day, I found some bumblebees
That bumbled around in a flower bed.
I sat right down where they bumbled in
And scooped them up, with the screw-on lid.

Then I listened to them buzz, inside that glass jar,
When I shook and I shook that BUZZING jar hard,
And I heard them say, "Let me out!" "Let me free!"
When through the lid hole, one bee stung me!

Rick L. Williams, Ph.D.

Beautiful Butterflies

Among the flowers in farms of green
A beautiful butterfly fluttered by me.
A wingspan full of marvelous colors
With it's long thorax, above me hovered.

To my surprise it landed now
Upon my arm and hand somehow.
As if to say, "Admire me."
It stood right there for all to see.

The sections of its wings all lined
With blackened shades so very fine.
And gleaming in the bright sunlight,
Were yellow and orange, to my delight!

(Poem Continues)

Then many more surrounded me
As I quietly sat among the trees.
And paying no mind to me or care,
They kept on pollinating flowers there.

God's birds and bees just buzzed on by
Across the fields and clouded skies.
But butterflies they stayed with me
To flit and flutter, so Heavenly.

Genesis 1:21 King James Version (KJV)
21 And God created great whales, and every living
creature that moveth, which the waters brought forth
abundantly, after their kind, and every winged fowl after
his kind: and God saw that it was good.

Genesis 1:10 King James Version (KJV)
10 And God called the dry land Earth; and the gathering together of the waters called he Seas: and God saw that it was good.

CHAPTER 3

I WALKED WITH GOD

ALONG THE SEA

Rick L. Williams, Ph.D.

Matthew 4:18 King James Version (KJV)
18 And Jesus, walking by the sea of Galilee, saw two
brethren, Simon called Peter, and Andrew his brother,
casting a net into the sea: for they were fishers.

I Walked Along the Beach with God

I walked along the beach with God,
To laugh and cry, that's not so odd.
Because I tell Him everything,
My life and dreams that I like sharing.

We chat as seagulls pass us by,
And waves rush in when the tide is high.
We chat as strong winds fiercely blow,
And the waves go out when the tide is low.

(Poem Continues)

God listens to my dreams and needs,
My hopes and all my harebrained schemes.
We laugh at some ideas I share.
God even cries to show he cares.

He's my best friend and like the beach,
There's just no end to where we reach.
I admire marvels that come into view,
He answers back, "One marvel is you."

I love the time we have alone.
Along the surf and ocean foam.
My spirit always gets a lift,
As I walk along God's beach like this.

Genesis 32:12 King James Version (KJV)

12 And thou saidst, I will surely do thee good, and make thy seed as the sand of the sea, which cannot be numbered for multitude.

Rick L. Williams, Ph.D.

Sea Waves

The sea, its waves they call to me.
They rise and fall repeatedly.
An endless, watery, sweet refrain,
Like God's own voice that calls my name.

The ocean's deep with its currents strong.
That make big waves when the water slows down.
To form great crests of impending doom,
That crash to shore in white-bubbling foam.

Beach sand it brings, when the tide's running high.
The waves grow louder, as they come crashing by.
Pushing the sand and the shells up so high,
To wet my feet now, and make me just smile.

(Poem Continues)

Ecclesiastes 1:7 King James Version (KJV)
7 All the rivers run into the sea; yet the sea is not full; unto the place from whence the rivers come, thither they return again.

Rick L. Williams, Ph.D.

Isaiah 48:18 King James Version (KJV)
18 O that thou hadst hearkened to my commandments! then had thy peace been as a river, and thy righteousness as the waves of the sea:

Experience God

I jump right in and splash in fun,
Into cold water, bright with sun.
The sand's so soft and the water's clear,
The seashore is a paradise here.

I rest under cool palm-tree shade,
Along the beach, with crashing waves.
The Sun sinks into God's own drink.
And boils seawater, it must, I think.

Genesis 1:5 King James Version (KJV)
5 And God called the light Day, and the darkness he
called Night. And the evening and the morning were the
first day.

Seaside Sunrise

Seaside sunrise so bright and new,
Brings God's light to me and you.
It breaks quite suddenly across the sky,
Illuminates our hearts and minds.

A new day dawns, waves crash by too,
They never stopped, the whole night through.
But now they sparkle bright and new,
With scattered light, in shades of blue.

Morning sunrise warms this new day,
The cold of the night has gone away.
Seagulls beckon as crabs scamper by,
They must find food or else they die.

(Poem Continues)

Proverbs 4:18 King James Version (KJV)
18 But the path of the just is as the shining light, that shineth more and more unto the perfect day.

Experience God

The sunlight now reveals what's new,
The water's erasing my footprints too.
The horizon's ablaze--so brilliantly lit.
It's so blindingly bright, I squint just a bit.

God has brought me a brand new day,
To cherish life in every way.
And like the sunrise, warm and kind,
I'll let my own love continually shine.

Rick L. Williams, Ph.D.

Collecting Seashells

Collecting seashells along the seashore,
Some broken ones found, I love even more.
They're smooth from the sand and hard pounding waves,
They're weathered great storms and darkened days.

But shells are quite bright, a child's delight,
Like pearls of yellow and those of white.
Once were alive with crusty green stems,
Now they're polished into seaside gems.

The beauty displayed is unique and rare,
They were all so rough, but now are fair.
A beauty, that's rich beyond all compare,
For those who dare to be different out there.

(Poem Continues)

Matthew 6:21 King James Version (KJV)
21 For where your treasure is, there will your heart be also.

Rick L. Williams, Ph.D.

Each groove and each ring that they proudly display,
Show colors so deep and nice shades of gray.
Some long shells, some short shells, they all are so nice,
Some thin ones, some fat ones; all will entice.

Now my collection of seashells is really neat,
Since I have *this* one, my treasure's complete.
But wait, just a moment now, I see one more,
"Just one more seashell!" I beg and implore.

Proverbs 8:21 King James Version (KJV)
21 That I may cause those that love me to inherit
substance; and I will fill their treasures.

Matthew 4:19 King James Version (KJV)
19 And he saith unto them, Follow me, and I will make
you fishers of men.

Gone Fishing by the Sea

Gone fishing now down by the sea,
I cast my line in front of me.
And set it up along in the sand
To catch a fish, I know I can.

I keep a finger on a line,
Enjoy the surf and bide my time.
Eventually I feel a jerk,
And then my face it breaks a smirk.

For I have hooked a fish that's fine.
But I wonder exactly just what kind?
Striped sea bass, a blue, or flounder that hid?
I fished with clam bellies and a nice piece of squid.

(Poem Continues)

Rick L. Williams, Ph.D.

It must be so big, it pulls hard on the line
With such a strong force--all of the time.
I try to reel it in, it's so very hard,
The line I just cast is out very far.

At last the sea monster, it comes into view,
With tentacles of green, and saltwater blue.
But It's not a fish to my utter dismay,
It's seaweed and kelp that's come by my way.

Genesis 1:26 King James Version (KJV)

26 And God said, Let us make man in our image, after our likeness: and let them have dominion over the fish of the sea, and over the fowl of the air, and over the cattle, and over all the earth, and over every creeping thing that creepeth upon the earth.

Rick L. Williams, Ph.D.

Mighty Storms at Sea

A storm at sea, a hurricane,
A mighty gale is now to blame,
For destructive waves and pounding surf,
That challenge me for all I'm worth.

Destroying boats and stores and homes,
Along the shore with white sea foam.
The tide comes higher and rushes in
To take back the beach where I have been.

The sea reclaims all that is its own.
Redraws the coastline that it's just loaned.
To oceanfront homes and boardwalk streets,
They're always in danger from storms at sea.

The storms at sea will return once again,
To take what is hers and she knows no friend.
So lighthouse keepers, you all must be,
Beware the mighty storms at sea.

Isaiah 28:2 King James Version (KJV)
2 Behold, the Lord hath a mighty and strong one, which as a tempest of hail and a destroying storm, as a flood of mighty waters overflowing, shall cast down to the earth with the hand.

Coral Reefs

When the coral reefs come into view
Below the sea in front of you
You're amazed by underwater life you see;
The fish, the coral, the anemones.

In every color and pattern around,
Swim yellowtail snappers and fish like clowns.
Striped bass and perch just float on by,
While sharks give you their evil eye.

The minnows peek from coral reefs
With crabs and octopuses that creep.
Coral, alive with things that squirm
Are thousands of tiny aquatic life forms.

(Poem Continues)

Genesis 1:22 King James Version (KJV)
22 And God blessed them, saying, Be fruitful, and
multiply, and fill the waters in the seas, and let fowl
multiply in the earth.

Rick L. Williams, Ph.D.

They live and build upon the reef
Great colonies that lie beneath.
Beneath these waves the plankton thrives,
The coral reef is so alive.

God's underwater paradise
Where creatures live all day and night,
They carry on life's chain beneath
The ocean blue on coral reefs.

Matthew 13:47 King James Version (KJV)
47 Again, the kingdom of heaven is like unto a net, that was cast into the sea, and gathered of every kind:

Matthew 14:33 King James Version (KJV)
33 Then they that were in the ship came and worshiped him, saying, Of a truth thou art the Son of God.

Key West Evening Sunset Cruise

A Key West evening sunset cruise,
Has skies of pink, yellow, and blue.
It's just the place to admire the Sun,
In southern skies, when the day is done.

A trip, ten miles out, with no land around
Is like Heaven on Earth when the Sun goes down.
This yellow-burning ball of light
Dips down below, then out of sight.

And I can hear the ocean boil
Like fried clam strips dropped into oil,
When this fiery ball descends,
No land in sight on the horizon.

(Poem Continues)

Mark 6:51 King James Version (KJV)
51 And he went up unto them into the ship; and the wind ceased: and they were sore amazed in themselves beyond measure, and wondered.

And moments then after it's all gone,
The Earth refracts the light along.
It bends around the planet's curve
With reds and pinks, and orange; I've learned.

A most spectacular sunset to see
With no obstructions, no buildings or trees.
The clouds above--a colorful rush
Like strokes of paint from God's airbrush.

Psalm 92:12 King James Version (KJV)
12 The righteous shall flourish like the palm tree: he shall grow like a cedar in Lebanon.

God's Palm-Tree Lessons

Palm trees they grow in climates hot,
Among the beaches and ocean spots.
They've learned how to weather life's storms
By bending, swaying--back and forth.

And on a hot and humid day
They shield the ground with lots of shade.
And you can make most anything
From tropic palms. They're amazing.

Palm baskets, shades, crosses, and rings,
Palm roses, rugs, palm mats, and slings.
You can cut them, bend them, and fold them too.
There seems no limit to what palms can do.

(Poem Continues)

John 12:13 King James Version (KJV)
13 Took branches of palm trees, and went forth to meet him, and cried, Hosanna: Blessed is the King of Israel that cometh in the name of the Lord.

Through palms, God shows us many things
Which way to go. What you can be.
Surviving when life seems too tough,
When it's too hot or you've had enough.

So have strong roots, know where you belong,
Be flexible enough to weather life's storms.
Stand tall, with your eyes always fixed on God,
God's palm-tree lessons leave me in awe.

John 21:6 King James Version (KJV)

6 And he said unto them, Cast the net on the right side of the ship, and ye shall find. They cast therefore, and now they were not able to draw it for the multitude of fishes.

Digging for Clams

We walked right down to the side of the bay,
When the tide was out and the water's low
To dig for muscles and clams, right there
In the saltwater reeds and muck below.

The muscle bed, at the foot of the reeds
Was very close to the edge of the shore,
So we waded out in our bathing suits,
And pulled them up in handfuls galore.

We found the clams with sneakers on our feet,
They felt like little rocks on the floor of the sea.
We walked like this, along the bottom of the bay
The water's only about two feet, anyway.

(Poem Continues)

And when we stepped on a rock or a clam
We reached underwater to feel with our hand.
For the shape and curve of a quahog clam,
Not flat, but curved with ridges all around.

Then we picked up the clam, with just our bare hands,
From the mud, and the clay and the saltwater sand.
And when we pulled one up from the mud and the goop,
There were more to be had for clams hide in groups.

John 21:10 King James Version (KJV)
10 Jesus saith unto them, Bring of the fish which ye have now caught.

Rick L. Williams, Ph.D.

Full Moon over Miami

The Miami moon so full and bright,
Reflected in the black and white
Of dark and rising ocean waves
That crash to shore with cliffs and caves.

Illuminates the water scape
Romantic honeymoon escapes.
It's tidal power from above
Are mirrored in your eyes, my love.

The ocean moon above the sea
Amazes me and sets us free
To think it's there for only us
Our private light of love and trust.

God sent the moon for us to view
His firmament above the blue
Holds promises in full moonlight
For lasting love, that shines tonight.

And like the moonlit ocean sky,
Your love shines bright into my eyes.
A sweet romantic love's embrace,
This moonlit love upon your face.

Genesis 37:9 King James Version (KJV)
9 And he dreamed yet another dream, and told it his brethren, and said, Behold, I have dreamed a dream more; and, behold, the sun and the moon and the eleven stars made obeisance to me.

John 14:2 King James Version (KJV)
2 In my Father's house are many mansions: if it were not so, I would have told you. I go to prepare a place for you.

Newport Cliff Walk

The Cliff Walk winds past surf and sand,
By big mansions in Rhode Island.
The huge waves crash far down below
From ocean seas so blue and cold.

The marble mansions adorned with gold
Display the wealth from days of old
When Vanderbilts and Astors too
Built cottages along Belevue.

Unlike the cliffs so wild and free,
The mansions' gates, like prisons keep
The riches of a yesteryear
Locked up. So please don't get too near.

KEEP OUT! These private domiciles,
Where tax-free structures climb so high.
But their majestic stained glass fails
When to His rocks and seas, compared.

For man's attempt to hoard wealth dies
When God calls from the other side.
Real wealth is still His crashing seas,
His bright sunrise, and ocean breeze.

God's house has many mansions too.
And He's prepared a place for you.
Just like the cliffs and seas, it beckons.
The House of God eternal in the heavens.

Rick L. Williams, Ph.D.

ABOUT THE AUTHOR

Dr. Williams is a faithful, insightful, and gifted poet, musician, dancer, artist, writer, mathematician, engineer, and educator. He possesses a unique talent for expressing his own personal and inspired walk with God in original contemporary rhyming poetic verse. He is truly a renaissance man.

Rick first earned a Bachelor of Science degree in chemistry and he worked as an engineer in the electronics industry. He went on to pursue a new teaching and administrative career in education where he also earned a Bachelor Degree, Master's Degree, and his Ph.D.

Dr. Williams' devotion to gaining and sharing a Godly insight with others has been exemplified by his own pursuits as a Sunday school teacher, a public school teacher, and a chaplain in the Masonic Order. God's Word is the moral compass for his life.

His quest for creative accomplishments has inspired him as a writer, singer, dancer, educator, DJ, wedding videographer, and photographer, decorator, motorcyclist, convertibles and racing enthusiast, as well as his pursuits in boating, water skiing, zip lining, and fishing.

Dr. Williams also enjoys creating works of 3-D IMVU avatar graphics, digital movies, slide shows, working on muscle cars, and building his own computers.

Follow all Dr. Williams' books and videos, along with his many author reading and author signing events on his websites: www.facebook.com/drlovepoems, www.pinterest.com/drlovepoems, http://www.twitter.com/drlovepoems, www.instagram.com/drrickwilliams, www.tumblr.com/drrickwilliams, www.youtube.com

Dr. Williams can also be contacted on this email:
drlovepoems@gmail.com
Books available at Amazon.com and Barnes & Noble, both online and in stores near you.

Made in the USA
Monee, IL
29 July 2021